# Beneath the Surface of Change

## FIVE ESSENTIAL ELEMENTS FOR INCREASING PRODUCTIVITY

### INCLUDING: SKUBA FOR DIVING INTO CHANGE

BY

Randy McClure

ISBN: 978-1-4251-6950-3

 www.trafford.com

**North America & international**
toll-free: 1 888 232 4444 (USA & Canada)
phone: 250 383 6864 ♦ fax: 250 383 6804 ♦ email: info@trafford.com

**The United Kingdom & Europe**
phone: +44 (0)1865 722 113 ♦ local rate: 0845 230 9601
facsimile: +44 (0)1865 722 868 ♦ email: info.uk@trafford.com

10 9 8 7 6 5 4 3 2

# Beneath the Surface of Change

## FIVE ESSENTIAL ELEMENTS FOR INCREASING PRODUCTIVITY

# Contents

**A Suggested Reading List:**

Jim Collins
*Good to Great*

Alan P. Brache
*How Organizations Work*

Peter Han
*Nobodies to Somebodies*

Tom Kelley and Jonathan Littman
*The Ten Faces of Innovation*

James O'Toole and Edward E. Lawler III
*The New American Workplace*

Tom Moore
*Developing a Competitive Advantage in Human Capital*

Stephen M.R. Covey with Rebecca Merrill
*The Speed of Trust*

# About the Author

Mr. McClure earned both a bachelor of science in Business Administration and an M.B.A. graduating with honors, from Oklahoma City University. After a 25 year career in sales and operations in the healthcare and manufacturing sectors he currently consults with companies in the area of business process improvement and organizational development. His diverse consulting experience includes utilities, healthcare, energy and public education. He is an adjunct instructor at Rogers State University, College of Business and Technology, and teaches Principles of Management and Organizational Behavior. Mr. McClure serves on the education committee for the Tulsa Metro Chamber of Commerce and is active in the small business council. He also is a member of the Oklahoma Business and Education Coalition.

# *Preface*

In light of near zero growth in earnings, Tom Osenton points out in his book, *The Death of Demand* (Prentice-Hall, Inc., 2004) that corporations still failed to find gains in productivity after three decades of pressure to show improvement. The result of this pressure to improve productivity and cut costs has been an unending search for that "perfect program" or method that provides the way for corporations to meet their financial goals. The search for these improvements has forced constant interruptions in the workplace. Interruptions came in the form of new programs to reduce operating expenses and these programs were generally accepted on the surface as useful and good for the organization, but under the surface they caused anxiety and heartache among workers who rarely had the "benefits" of the program communicated.

In the 1980s, the quest for growing company top-line revenues changed to one where it was acceptable to show a company's growth in what they earned. In other words, reduced expenses became more important than revenue—growth in revenues became nearly non-existent.

A company's earnings drive its stock price; High earnings encourage the market to invest in it which provides the funds for acquiring the revenue growth needed to survive. From the growth that is acquired, the increased revenues make way for company divisions to merge operations and reduce costs, which should provide the coveted earnings growth. Without revenue growth, markets will experience cutbacks resulting in people losing their jobs, a slowdown or hold on activity in research and development (R&D) of new products, and in most cases a reduction in the price of the company's stock. A lower stock price puts even more pressure on ways to reduce expenses.

Today, productivity gains are a more politically correct way to discuss how a company may show an increase without bringing attention to the fact that the top-line is decreasing. Getting fewer workers to produce more is the only way that a company shows progress in this category. The reduction in revenues has also made relationships with customers more important than ever.

The potential end of reducing expenses is to cannibalize the quality of the corporation's product or service. (There is only so much that can be cut.) There comes a point where one must turn out the lights and go home because the reality is that there are economic floors and ceilings when considering cutting costs and gaining revenue growth. How can we change it all?

When it comes to change, the Italian philosopher Machiavelli

(1469–1527), a key figure of the Italian Renaissance and a central figure of its political component most widely known for his treatises on realist political theory, said it best:

> "It must be remembered that there is nothing more difficult to plan, more doubtful of success, nor more dangerous to manage than the creation of a new system. For the initiator has the enmity of all who would profit by the preservation of the old institutions, and merely lukewarm defenders in those who would gain by the new ones."

*Introduction*

## CONFRONTING THE CATALYST OF CHANGE

Organizational success requires an environment where employees know to take ownership in their performance, creating operational excellence and stakeholder value. For employees to improve or change at the organizational level they must be able to align themselves at the individual level with corporate-level goals. This personal accountability will occur when conditions in their working environment promote learning and personal growth and when the organization is structured to promote good relationships between employers, employees and customers.

If ever you have been involved in implementing a new program or new way of doing work that made your audience (employees, constituents, volunteers, etc.) feel the pain of change, you will appreciate this book. Whether on the receiving end or on the end of *implementation-gone-wrong*, the pain of poorly executed change is real and the memories are long lasting.

All businesses, from small firms to large corporations, experience moments when sustainable change is necessary to reach established goals. This book is a framework for what you already know. It addresses the leadership who is responsible for corporate change, but its application also offers guidance to individuals wanting to survive changes in the workplace. Individuals who feel valuable to their corporation will make the corporation valuable to its customers. That is why it is critical for leadership to involve their associates in necessary changes.

To find ongoing success in the workplace, all levels of associates must continuously ask the question, "Who do I need to be in order to meet the need of this company, and what does this company need to be to meet the need of the customer"? In other words, it is necessary for both management and personnel to transform how they respond to the needs of others as the needs of others continue to change.

This book is a synthesis of my personal experiences as a management consultant and thoughts about business situations that have taken place over twenty-five years. In this book, I will show that success is _not_ only gained through better use of technology, organizational psychology, or improvement methodology, but through a framework of response to change for all three. It is _not_ suggested that Organizational Behavior theory be ignored, rather, the concepts in this book link the theoretical to the func-

RANDY McCLURE

tional. What you learn from this book will apply to any organization no matter its purpose.

I have instructed numerous members of organizations how to acquire successful skills to achieve positive change. My intention is to deliver a quick and easy read for any leader facing the challenge of operational / organizational changes in their business. But, if you are an individual who aspires to be more valuable in your workplace, you will also benefit from the information shared in this book.

Owners and managers must continually reduce complexity and the cost of quality. They must also build confidence in their firm's level of performance. Concerns over developing good leaders in their firms, looking for ways to improve the bottom line, or planning how to increase top-line revenue are just some of the daily challenges.

As a manager, you will better understand and value the people working with you toward your corporate goals. If you are an associate reporting to leadership that is sometime vague and lacks good communication skills, you will enjoy this book for its helpful instruction on how to adapt in the workplace and make yourself more valuable to the company you serve.

In the final chapter, I will illustrate composites of employees who get it. "It" being an understanding that responding to change is not something we do only once, but how we respond to change is the way we do everything effectively. Every moment involves change. Every morning when we get up, there is change. Every time we buy something, we have made a change in our situation. Every time we meet someone our lives change. Every time we learn something new, do something new, or think about something in a different light, we experience change. So it's not that we don't like change—it is being *told that we must change* that we resist.

An acronym used in this book is SKUBA. The idea of SKUBA (Seeking, Knowing, Understanding, Believing, and Acting) was developed as a learning tool while I was teaching at Rogers State University (a regional university in northeast Oklahoma). Out of frustration over low student exam scores, I first utilized the idea as an experimental team-based learning guide for students to complete projects meant to stretch them and get them extra credit.

As an instructor, I did not feel low exam scores were because the information had not been available to the students, rather it was the fact they were not giving their projects critical thought—they were not taking ownership. Therefore, it was not relevant to them. After introducing the concepts in SKUBA, the response was astonishing. Students told me they learned how to think like managers by applying this system more than by traditional text and lecture methods. Here's what a few of my students wrote:

> "Going through this process is more than just learning the principles of management. It gave me the confidence to approach any situation, and know that I can handle it—even if I don't have all the details."
>
> —*T. M., RSU student, 2005*

> "This project helped me realize what it takes to be a good manager and realize that you need to get employees involved to create a successful environment. I am really glad that I had the opportunity to take this class."
>
> —*A. K., RSU student, 2005*

"Thank you for the opportunity to discover what each of us is capable of individually, and as a team."

—*S. M. RSU student, 2005*

## OUTSIDE PRESSURE ON ORGANIZATIONS

In their book, *Innovation,* Curtis Carlson and William Wilmot discuss how, competition is changing businesses. A global economy means that competitors are as likely to come from across the ocean as from across town. Heightened competition also makes it necessary for established organizations to defend themselves against both traditional competitors, who develop new products and services, and small, entrepreneurial firms with innovative offerings. Technology is changing work and organizations. Cell phones that replace IPODs and PDAs are increasingly perceived as necessities by a large segment of the population. Many companies are spending large amounts of money on training to upgrade the skills of their employees.

*Needs of the market* also change. At the time of this writing, a major clothing distributor announced lost revenues this past year. It was once the leading supplier for teens to twenty-something buyers, but something changed this past year. Their consumers were no longer seeking only jeans, polo shirts and T-shirts. New designers were being challenged, and the once extremely successful company is considering putting itself up for sale.

Improved communication in the employer/employee relationship is essential in managing response to change. By integrating the principles of organizational behavior with proven concepts in marketing, employees take ownership of vision and values and turn organizations into customer-focused machines.

Leadership should address change as an intentional, goal-oriented activity, and managers should present response activities that are proactive and purposeful. For example, ask employees what is the goal of responding to market pressures? Essentially there are two. The first is to improve the ability of the organization to adapt changes to its current environment. The second goal is to minimize resistance in the employee response to operational improvements.

If an organization is to survive and thrive it must respond to market pressures. An organization must adapt when competitors introduce new products or services, government agencies enact new laws, important sources of supply go out of business, or similar market changes take place.

Success or failure is essentially due to the things that employees do or fail to do. The purpose of leadership is to improve the performance of individuals and groups as well as processes within the organization. The key to successful change management is to know what *learning process* individuals must experience in order to embrace the change.

## KNOW THE OBSTACLES TO CHANGE

Stephen Roberts, author of *Organizational Behavior* (*Ninth Edition* Prentice-Hall, Inc., 2001), explains that resistance to change resides in the basic human characteristics of perceptions, personalities, and needs. He writes that the following six tendencies summarize reasons that individuals may resist change.

*Habit*: As human beings, we are creatures of habit. Life is complex enough: we don't need to consider the full range of options for the hundreds of decisions we have to make every day. To cope with this complexity, we all rely on habits or programmed responses. But when confronted with change, this tendency to respond in our normal ways becomes a source of resistance.

*Security*: People with high insecurity are likely to resist change because it threatens their feelings of job security. Many employees are threatened if they feel their jobs are in jeopardy.

*Economic Factors*: Changes in job tasks or work routines can also cause economic fears if people feel inadequate to perform the new tasks or routines to their previous standards, especially when pay is closely tied to productivity.

*Fear of the Unknown*: Changes introduce ambiguity and uncertainty. When you trade the known for the unknown, you increase fear or insecurity. Employees in organizations hold the same dislike for uncertainty. If, for example, the introduction of quality management means production workers will have to learn statistical process control techniques, some may fear they will be unable to do so. They may develop a negative attitude toward a quality management program or disrupt the function if required to use statistical methods.

*Selective Information Processing*: Individuals selectively process information in order to keep their perceptions intact. They hear only what they want to hear. They may ignore the arguments their managers make in explaining why having knowledge of statistical methods is necessary for the potential benefits the change will provide for them.

*Interpreting Change*: A key element in effectively communicating the change is knowing how your employees interpret change. Managers should identify the consequences and values that employees consider most important. Communication should be designed to activate those feelings and emotions that link positive consequences to the planned change. This will motivate employees to focus their attention on this information, interpret it more fully, and then act on it.

An example of how this works can be seen when marketers of *Sure* brand deodorant identified two self-relevant and emotionally motivating consequences of using their product: (1) social confidence, and (2) avoiding embarrassment. In a long-running campaign with the phrase, "Raise your hand if you're Sure", they communicated these psycho-social consequences in ads that showed coatless consumers in social situations raising their arms and not being embarrassed by damp spots on their clothing.

Comprehending change refers to the processes by which employees make sense of how the change will affect relevant aspects of their work. Most people are not comfortable with change, and when confronted with it, they automatically try to relate to it through past experiences, which may be partially relevant at best. Employees must develop an understanding of the change (or intentionally ignore it).

Deep comprehension produces more abstract meanings that result in the employee having greater comfort in vague or ambiguous situations. Deeper comprehension of change also produces meanings that are self-relevant. Shallow comprehension processes tend to produce meanings only about the change, rather than answers the employee's question, "What is the meaning for me in this change?" Simply put, the greater the perceived change, the greater the need for understanding.

Many factors influence whether or not an employee comprehends change. These factors affect the depth and elaboration of comprehension when employees interpret information. Their ability to comprehend information is largely determined by their existing knowledge in memory.

An employee's involvement in the communication process has a major influence on their motivation to comprehend informa-

RANDY McCLURE

tion. Employees who feel highly involved tend to form deeper meanings for the information. Those who experience low levels of involvement when exposed to information about change tend to find the information uninteresting and irrelevant, or at worst, disturbing.

In order to gain performance improvements, organizations should focus not only on *what* to change but also on *how* to respond to change. Employees need to understand and be involved in the process of a planned response to change. Before they will act to make changes happen, employees must be convinced that the change is right, reasonable, and know how it is relevant to their environment.

To effectively communicate response strategies, managers should use employee input to deliver information that will be interpreted correctly and help them to embrace the change. How? Experts agree that those who are closest to the work should be expected to look for ways to improve the way work is done. This only happens if workers in their areas of responsibility are given the tools to think like good managers.

Often times, the first response to improve performance is to look at operational processes that get us the changes we want in the appropriate performance indicators. These changes may be good in and of themselves. However, if changes are made but the forces that brought about the need for change are *not* dealt with, then sustaining the improvement is unlikely.

One very valuable principle I've learned while working with companies over the years is that sustained operational success comes through people who understand and embrace change associated with improving internal processes and technology.

# EQUIP YOUR EMPLOYEES

When an entire organization is focused on solving the most important customer needs, an exciting, empowering workplace is created. Motivating associates in the workplace to find innovative solutions and adapt to the need for change is not unlike the energy of a bouncing ball. We drop the ball and it bounces back according to the material it is made of, the density of the surface it is dropped on to, and the height from which it was dropped. Regardless of all those factors, the ball eventually reaches equilibrium and remains at rest.

This bouncing ball effect is similar to momentum in employees. They begin with a lot of potential (the height from which the ball is dropped), but they quickly reach equilibrium and become still if allowed (or encouraged by their peers or environment) to do so. Keeping valuable associates energized and productive is crucial to the success of any corporation.

To embrace and respond to change, both leaders and employees must have the appropriate skills and mindset to make successful change happen. The following pages will give you what I refer to as SKUBA gear to help you initiate change with confidence and accurate expectations for a positive outcome. SKUBA is my acronym for leading positive response to changes you want to incorporate in your business. You must direct yourself and inspire your employees and customers to: *Seek, Know, Understand, Believe and Act.*

We seek what we value.   I will help you *seek* "improvements". In response to the improvements we will plan for change and clearly communicate the plan so that everyone *knows* (acknowledges the agent of change) and *understands* why change is necessary and how it will affect them. Consequently you will win the support of your team, who must also *believe that the change is right and that the personal cost of the change is reasonable* so that they will finally *act* on the plan. Once you have your SKUBA gear in place, you will know how to equip your associates for diving in to new opportunities.

# 1

## Share Your Knowledge

The scenario: Steve pondered the recent sequence of undesirable events as he stared out of his office window. *I thought that by promoting Bob, he would see the benefit and stretch to reach for the next level of performance. Instead, he quit!* Steve stood up and paced the floor in front of his desk as his agitation increased. *What was he thinking? How could Bob just walk away from such an incredible opportunity?*

Suddenly, Steve's thoughts turned to the customer sales report on his desk. *And what happened to GETTCORP? They are a great customer. What went wrong there? What was it that we could not do for them? Does anybody know? Can anyone tell me? I need some answers.*

All of this was swirling around in Steve's head when he realized everything was changing and his company was missing something. He knew that something was wrong when a talented individual like Bob walked out the door in the face of what seemed to be a great opportunity (for him and for the company), and when good customers choose to do business with others who don't seem to have any more to offer than his own company. Was he right? You'll see more about how he arrived at these conclusions later—see if you agree with him. For now let's continue with thought of change from the manager's view.

Steve had always been able to find a way to fix any problem, or at least surround himself with talented associates who could focus on the task and get things straightened out. But this time was different. Steve sensed that more was needed than just throwing money or committee meetings at the problem until it was gone. And in this point, Steve was thinking clearly.

Like so many managers with whom I have consulted over the years, Steve was facing a deeper dimension of challenge than simple supply and demand. Steve needed to turn negative results to positive ones for his employees. To survive Steve's impending changes, Bob should have been included in the process of seeking solutions, knowing the best plan of action, and understanding the motives and purpose of the change, so that he could determine for himself whether they were the right steps. If Bob had been more involved in developing the plan he would have been more likely to take action on his part of the plan.

# WHAT CUSTOMERS SEE

What might have happened if Bob had been more involved in developing a plan for change that was going to affect him?

Imagine how good it would feel as a manager or owner of a company if your employees were mining (*seeking*) nuggets of information about your customers and their preferences on a continuous basis. What if your employees then took the data they found and made the customer information available across the entire organization in a meaningful way so that your firm could acknowledge (*knowing*) what you know about your customers and use that knowledge in all of their customer relationship activities?

And what if your employees understood your vision and strategy and linked that *understanding* to your company's business processes (the guts of what you do)? Think of the value an individual would have who has this understanding and *believes* in both your vision and strategy. What if all employees believed that the new way you want them to do their work (value-add processes) made sense in that it seems both the right way to do things and reasonable in the way of expectations for outcomes in order to meet your customer's needs?

The truth is employees will only act (*acting*) on what they *believe*. I'm not referring to actions like showing up on time and trading work-time for dollars and clocking out only to forget that day's activities and to repeat the same mindless game tomorrow, but action in the sense that all employees have unique talents, personalities, experiences, and values through which they *interpret and translate the essence of a firm to its customers*. Customers don't necessarily see the corporate vision, processes, or tasks— they only see how all that "internal stuff" is interpreted and then *relayed through employees* (those with whom they make contact).

Consider your own workplace and evaluate the following questions:

- How effectively is each employee interpreting what they know about your customers and your company's vision and strategy for meeting their needs?

- How is information about the customer's needs integrated into the planning process and then synthesized with the corporate vision/strategy at the worker level?

- How is this information linked into the business processes through which your employees are completing the tasks?

- Do you as a leader have a good understanding of these steps?

- Do your employees get it? If they understand, then the customer does too. If they don't understand what your company has to offer, then the customer will only be offered whatever portion of value they are able to pass along to them.

- What percentage of the whole do your employees know?

- What is it costing you (the owner/manager) when your employees lack understanding of your business plan?

After answering these questions do you see that what Bob did by quitting was created by a lack of understanding of the corporate goals and his part in the bigger picture? Does it make sense that customers see the results of what employees know and understand about corporate goals and their respective role in achieving those goals?

## FIVE ELEMENTS FOR ORGANIZATIONAL IMPROVEMENT

The *five elements of organizational improvement* are seeking, knowing, understanding, believing, and acting (SKUBA).

These are attributes that govern the way people perceive and respond to the difference between their current-state circumstances and expected changes (or improvements) in their future-state circumstances. To personalize it: what is it going to be like when we change and what do you see my role in the new way of doing things?

Managers reduce resistance to change by knowing the five SKUBA elements and their *functional* and *psycho/social consequences*. From a functional perspective it must be determined what structure should be in place in order to deliver the education and training necessary for employees to be good "consumers" of what it is you want them to do. And from a psycho/social viewpoint you should determine how to appeal to employees' thoughts, feelings, and values in order to get them to take ownership in what it is you want them to do. Take the risk of sharing what you know in order to broaden the understanding of your associates and in so doing, you will reduce your risk of losing customers. So let's take a deeper look at managing your risks.

## CHAPTER ONE - ACTIVITY

This survey tool is adapted from Don Hellriegel & John Slocum in their book: Organizational Behavior, 10/e (Thompson-Southwestern, Inc., 2004) and is designed to help you understand the level of support or opposition to change within an organization. You may want to complete the survey yourself and then have others complete it for a comparison in perspectives.

**Score each survey question in the following way:**
Not True = 1; Usually Not True = 2; Somewhat Not True = 3; Neutral = 4; Somewhat True = 5; Usually True = 6; True = 7

## SURVEY QUESTIONS

### Values and Vision
1. Do people throughout the organization share val-     Score: _____
ues or vision?

### History of Change
2. Does the organization have a good track record     Score: _____
in implementing change smoothly?

### Cooperation and Trust
3. Is there a lot of cooperation and trust throughout     Score: _____
the organization (as opposed to animosity)?

### Culture
4. Does the organization's culture support risk     Score: _____
taking (as opposed to being highly bureaucratic
and rule bound)?

### Resilience
5. Are people able to handle change (as opposed to     Score: _____
being worn out from recent changes)?

### Punishments and Rewards
6. Does the organization reward people who take     Score: _____
part in change efforts (as opposed to punishing
those who try but fail)

### Respect and Status
7. Will people be able to maintain respect and     Score: _____
status when the change is implemented As op-
posed to losing them as a result of change)?

### Status Quo
8. Will the change be mild (and not cause disrup-     Score: _____
tion of the status quo)?

RANDY McCLURE

**Values and Vision** – low scores may indicate values are in conflict and that individuals and groups may not perceive any common ground. Communication needs to be improved.

**History of Change** – low scores indicate likelihood that change will be resisted forcefully. People are likely to be skeptical.

**Cooperation and Trust** – the opposite of trust is fear so a low score indicates not only the absence of trust but also the presence of fear.

**Culture** – the change agents must be willing to look at reward systems and procedures in order to facilitate change.

**Resilience** – depends on two questions: 1. Is change necessary at this time, and 2. If yes, how can we minimize disruption? Low scores may indicate people are burned out.

**Punishments and Rewards** – change agents must find ways to make change rewarding for others. Low scores indicate a misunderstanding about the scope and reasons for change.

**Respect and Status** – low scores mean change agents must find ways to make change a win-win.

**Status Quo** – the more involved people are in the change process the less resistance you are likely to experience.

# 2

## *Manage Your Organizational Risk*

*Risk* takes many different forms. The following examples illustrate unwanted results that may occur if your employees are not prepared for change. The list may be quite familiar, and this is not an exhaustive list.

*Damaged Public Image:* The first risk you may be taking is in the potential loss of business through your employees' mistranslation or misinterpretation of your corporate goals and values. Ask yourself:

1.  Are my customers getting the same point of view of

my company that they would if they talked directly to me every time they had contact with my company?

2. Are things always being done or handled the way I would do it, or the way I would want it done? The way it should be done?

3. If not, what is this costing me with my customers?

*Operational Efficacy*: Risk also comes in the form of operational efficacy such that it is desirable that any mistakes made in the value-add process be moved upstream as far as possible. By upstream, I mean that potential mistakes should be caught at a point farthest away from the customer. Think about the costs involved in shipping a faulty product to a customer and having it be noticed only upon their need to use the product. The cost of that mistake is huge both in financial terms as well as in terms of goodwill. In theory, early detection of faulty products reduces the cost of additional mistakes with fewer departments/fewer people involved.

*System Noise*: Noise is a curious term to me, but suitable in that the way noise is perceived by the owner, manager or employee can be the variation, dissonance, or difference between the desired way (the way things should be) and the way things actually are—and this noise, although not audible, can be annoying.

A practical example of noise in the system might be department supervisors or managers who continually point fingers at others when they do not meet performance expectations (forecast). They whine or complain that the "other" department, manager, etc., is not getting them their information/supplies on time and therefore *blah blah blah* . . . It's the external locus of control where one blames their circumstances on others or variables beyond their control. The "locus" is

RANDY McCLURE

simply where control resides. It either resides inside a person where they feel responsible for themselves and their behavior, or it resides outside where these individuals feel that circumstances and environment and other external issues actually control their destiny.

Another example of noise is where employees want to improve the current work flow, but all they do is complain about the way things *are* done. This happens if management is not structured to take critical input and understand how to use it in order to improve your company.

Noise happens when employees feel that no one who can improve their situation is listening, so they grumble about their inefficient computer system or complain that certain procedures seem to be a waste of time. The worst that can happen through this risk is that their "noise" goes beyond the office and affects customers or even potential future employees. Ignoring or downplaying the importance of employee input is very expensive.

Eventually, employees will go around a problem to get things done in ways that seem more efficient, or at least better for them. When they do this without corporate involvement, the borders between departments fade with no clear distinction of who handles which tasks. Departmental responsibilities become blurred when individuals within the company bear the risk of meeting customer needs on their own to reduce their own internal noise; before you know it, someone is doing the partial work of two or three people just to be able to get their own work done. Meanwhile, other departments suffer because they are out of the loop on certain processes performed without their knowledge.

# INVOLVED EMPLOYEES REDUCE RISK AND NOISE

If an employee is allowed to take ownership in what he does by having some reasonable level of power to influence how a task gets done, then he is more likely to share the risk of change. The role must be perceived as it fits into the overall scheme, but, because he is involved in the changes, the employee is more likely to own and manage the risk in the process. By engaging employees to find a solution to part of the process, the noise level will decrease because you have satisfied the psycho-social consequences of meeting felt needs.

If noise is left unchecked with employees, unwanted consequences are predictable. You will eventually be managing some or all of the following results:

- Turnover
- Absenteeism
- Complaints about compensation and/or benefits
- Low productivity or efficiency—("I can't get it all done. I've got to have help!")
- Trading hours for pay—not fully engaged—just putting in the time
- Attitudes not conducive to collaboration—"Doesn't do any good. Nothing ever changes."
- Customer complaints—or worse, no complaint except to other potential customers
- Finger pointing / blame between departments for low performance

- Silo or fiefdom mentality—up and down the chain of command, and for what?

- Grapevine is the primary communication source – where real organizational information comes through unofficial sources

- Work gets pushed off the plate without upstream/downstream consideration

- Unable to articulate the vision or mission of the company, department, or team

- Complaints of unfair practices for internal promotions

- No real decisions made for fear of retribution

- Unable to articulate role-fit within context of overall picture

- Superficial Company Guy - Talking a good game but not truly supportive of corporate goals

## LEARN FROM EXPERIENCE

How many of the previous symptoms are evident in your company? In the early nineties I personally experienced a particular corporate culture where people did the minimum amount of work with the maximum amount of lip service. Departments were silos where only top managers heard the directives from above—in the clouds where the executives lived. Those employees at the bottom of the silos were not given information because they were not considered to be contributors; in fact, they were not allowed to voice any ideas, they were simply to do as told.

Most employees were not even cognizant of the concept of making a contribution to the success of the organization. Besides, they were all looking for better paying jobs. The jobs that posted inside the company were only available to those who had some connection to the people in the department or by chance had some previous outside contact (which was rare) with the hiring manager. The rest scanned the employment section of the newspaper and posted their résumés on popular employment search sites on the Internet.

Almost all the employees below managers and supervisors worked second jobs. It was the norm for those dealing directly with the customers to be the lowest paid group in the company. Even with a bonus plan, none of the employees were motivated to achieve beyond the minimum expectations because if they exceeded the forecast one quarter, the compensation was structured where it only meant their sales expectations would become more difficult the next quarter.

When management tried to re-structure the bonus program so that it was compliance driven, in other words the min/max level became the target rather than customer-driven values, it backfired! By meeting the min/max compliance levels the bonuses paid out through the roof, but the customer complaints were directly proportionate. The point here is that employees worked to meet management's expectation only—not the customer's needs. Management quickly changed back to its original methods and the departments settled back into the comfort zone of mediocre performance.

Month after month, new employees and new casualties were processed through the human resource department. The cost of hiring and training one new employee was estimated at $40–$50,000. People would come and go regularly. When the company was already struggling to keep people motivated, they made an unfortunate decision to leave mainframe computing and upgrade to desktop PCs and servers. All hell broke loose and that decision only accelerated their downward spiral.

Without any live testing or parallel systems the decision was made to throw the switch to a new computer operating system and when they did, nothing happened—literally. For two solid months no orders, no invoices, no shipping documents, no receiving documents, not even sales orders were created, much less printed. Complete and utter chaos ruled. The interesting thing to me was how people reacted. Many people quit. They were not able to deal with the inconvenience of a crisis. To them this was the ultimate internal noise, and the noise was too loud.

Fast forward eight months from the crash. The president of the company had stepped down, an employee-satisfaction survey was administered, and incentives were offered to employees who could help the company find good people. Something else happened. The new president had a new way of thinking when it came to people who worked closest to the customers. In order to turn things around, he decided to hire outside management experts to help him.

After the first meeting with the management consultant, the employees caught a glimpse of hope that things might actually change for the better. For the first time, employees were invited to be a part of decisions that led to change, and change no longer had the negative connotation it had received in the past. Not surprisingly, employees were willing to take ownership in the necessary solutions and invest both emotionally and professionally in the way the company operated.

In department meetings, the expert asked employees if they would like to make existing procedures better, or shake the rug and start over again building the department into what it needed to be based on input from customer contact and the corporate vision.

One employee responded, "Whoa! Are you kidding me, we can do that?"

The expert said, "I don't know if you can or not, but if that is what you want to do I am here to help you and guide you on how to get it done." Most employees were captivated by the hope of positive change and felt it would be worth staying through the transitions. And shake the rug they did.

This company went on to experience double-digit growth throughout most of the next twelve years and continues to highly value its employees. And the noise level? It was gone almost immediately upon the employees realizing they were part of the positive change.

## CHAPTER TWO – ACTIVITY

*[Adapted from: Don Hellriegel & John Slocum in their book: Organizational Behavior, 10/e (Thompson-Southwestern, Inc., 2004)]*

Another tool for surveying work attitudes deals with job satisfaction and job-related behavior. They say that important sources of job satisfaction include the challenge of the job, interest in the kind of work performed, physical activity required, working conditions, rewards available from the organization and the nature of coworkers.

### MEASURE OF JOB SATISFACTION

Please indicate the extent of your satisfaction on the scale to each of the following statements.

A=Very dissatisfied; B=Dissatisfied; C=Cannot Decide; D=Satisfied; E=Very Satisfied

On my present job this is how I feel about . . .

_____ 1. Being able to stay busy all the time
_____ 2. The chance to be somebody in the organization
_____ 3. The way my job provides steady employment for me
_____ 4. My pay and the amount of work I do
_____ 5. The freedom to use my own thinking about how to do my work
_____ 6. The chance to work without anybody looking over me
_____ 7. The chance to develop close friendships with others
_____ 8. The way I get full credit for the work I do
_____ 9. The chance to help others when needed
_____ 10. My overall job security

High levels of dissatisfaction should be an indication to managers that problems exist with working conditions, reward systems, or the employee's role in the organization. In general, job satisfaction depends on the match between working conditions and physical needs. Working conditions that promote goal attainment and an environment where coworkers help people attain rewards are both satisfying and conducive to high self-esteem.

# 3

## *Refine Your "Operating" System*

Many managers deal with the same doubts and questions. They hear the example from chapter two and say, "Yeah that was great, but now what? How am I to understand this "noise" in my company (or department), and find out where it is coming from?"

Some managers sense the dissonance, but they don't know how to get to the source of the noise. Some may not want to start listening to employee suggestions out of fear of the enormity of chaos it could initiate. But they continue to hear the noise, and ignoring it will not bring anything positive to the workplace. Noise does not have to be at an audible level in order for you to be uncomfortable. Sensitive managers are alert to this undertone of discontent long before they can articulate where the problem may be breeding.

A leader may have good people, make good decisions, and provide good leadership for his staff, yet still sense the increase of noise. He may evaluate each staff member and feel confident they are on board with his ideas. He may demand a lot of his people but knows he is paying them as well as the next company and better than some of his competition. Perhaps he thinks everyone that works for him knows that he cares about them and want what's best for them. But still, he knows something is not quite right.

A manager I once worked with reasoned, "It does seem like any time we try something new, it is such a big deal just to get people to hear it and not react to it before they've given it a chance to work. But still, most everyone at least says they agree with new ideas once they have a chance to warm up to them and get over the fear of having to change something."

Then he explained how a previous program they had tried failed to survive past the first round of discussions. There was considerable confusion over it, and the project was never initiated. Yet, he didn't understand its failure because the new program had made complete sense to him when the vendor offering it made the pitch on why his company needed to make the improvement.

The vendor had even addressed how the new operating procedure would help the frontline people do things that would save them time and save the company money. But whatever the issue was that kept employees from accepting the new method, it never got past being just a good idea. The manager thought perhaps the timing of the proposal contributed to its rejection. After all, it came fairly close behind the first program they tried which had been a disaster. He admitted that he knew from the beginning they had a potential explosion on their hands, so he pulled the plug on this new project before any real damage occurred.

## STAY COMPATIBLE IN RESPONSE TO CHANGE

The attempts we make trying new programs is much like computers. We need to continually upgrade our computers in order to enjoy the ever-increasing benefits of new technology. Recently, I bought an application program for my "state-of-the-art" computer and when I tried to launch the program it would act for a moment as if it were going to execute and open, but shortly after the failed attempt, a message appeared that told me I could not run the program due to my operating system. My computer's operating system was not compatible with the application program and therefore it would not run.

Companies sometimes fail to get improvement programs off the ground, such as Six Sigma, Lean, Team-based management, changes in technology, or other improvement methodologies. Most likely, they do *not* have the correct "operating" system in place. The "operating" system in the case of a corporation is its operating environment, or the way the organization thinks. It is the dynamic of how a group of individuals think and feel collectively.

Making the analogy, when I bought the new application program for my computer, I had no intention of changing my entire operating system. After all, I was familiar with it and comfortable with how well it ran all of my other applications. The first time I launched the new program, it acted as if it would work, and then suddenly a message appeared that informed me that my current operating system would not run that particular application. Consequently, I never used that new application program. It became not important enough to me and my attention moved to other issues. It didn't make sense to change my entire operating system just to accommodate *one* application program. On the other hand, it wouldn't have been smart to continue buying applications that would not run on my current operating system. If there had been a middle-ground alternative, I probably would have given it consideration.

Some managers want their companies to change by adding new processes to old operating systems. They expect their "operating" system to be flexible, versatile and accommodate change according to their "new applications", but substantial change always requires new support systems. So, like an out-of-date computer, we should upgrade our platforms (the way we change) to improve our operations or be left behind.

Find a way to keep your employees enthusiastic about better ways to improve what they're doing and how they do it. Talking about new technology and streamlining production or services should be second nature to them. Make them feel that they are a different breed of innovative people. Initiate a safe atmosphere— an "operating" system that promotes good critical thinking.

You may think that creating such an environment is unrealistic in your business. You may be convinced the stress is so different on your employees, arguing that your customers, vendors, contractors, distributors, and even your competition adds too much pressure to take time to make changes. Perhaps you feel that you can't add time to research change to your already busy 12-plus hour day.

I often point out to doubtful managers that they already have at least one department operating the way everyone should be working. The Marketing and Sales departments understand every new quarter brings challenges from the marketplace. And thankfully, because they do keep focused on these challenges, they are keeping the company ahead of the competition—at least for now. So what gets Marketing and Sales people ready for challenge? How do they put up with changing their focus every quarter? They are the most accommodating, diverse, and flexible group in the corporate community.

Marketing and Sales people are asked to execute and run more programs (changes) in a year than anyone in the rest of the company, and somehow they pull it off. One motivation for this is that they get paid to feel good about change every quarter.

You may argue that you have other department managers that earn what salespeople earn, but they still are not near as willing to accept new ways of doing things. In fact, they complain every time you introduce any improvements as though it were the first time they experienced pain. Their "operating" system seems only to be able to run one program—status quo.

So is that the source of corporate noise? Are salespeople just different and able to adapt to new ideas easier than staff and frontline people? If it is not just compensation, what is it?

It isn't the amount of compensation that makes a difference in attitude between a salesperson and a bookkeeper in your company. The difference is salespeople *understand* that change is part of their job description for which they are compensated. Sales and Marketing people thrive on change—they understand that change is good. Change is meeting the needs of customers who are no longer satisfied with mundane, functional products or services. Customers are used to new ideas. If there isn't something new to buy this quarter, they will keep their money in their pockets. The rest of the corporation needs to understand that even though their applications may remain fundamental, they will succeed only when they can adapt their services to new "operating" systems—even as frequently as each new quarter.

Your employees will respond to their circumstances differently. Compensation may need to be considered, but if you are confident that compensation is not the issue keeping your employees in a rut of routine mediocrity, it is time to look at your "operating" system to gain more understanding of their lack of enthusiasm.

Refine your "operating" system so that everyone on board your company knows it is part of his or her job description to *seek* ways to improve. All associates should *know* why any proposed changes are necessary in a department and *understand* the cost/benefit of those changes. Once employees *understand* the perspective of management and/or corresponding departments, they will perform an internal check (asking themselves if the change is right for the situation) to see if they *believe* the cost/benefit is reasonable, and then *act* on it as well. This way, they will be able to adopt the change to the procedures of their own process. In the next chapter, we'll examine how to keep your "operating" system running quietly like a well-oiled machine.

## CHAPTER THREE – ACTIVITY

It does not matter whether your company is structured around hierarchy and chain-of-command, division of labor, span of control, or policy and procedure. What does matter is whether you have systems in place that create an environment containing these five functional consequences of structure:

1. Channels for information, communication and learning about the business

2. Relationships and interaction around how work gets done

3. A process for employee engagement with input into the discovery process of the desired end result of change

4. Recognition and reward systems that positively reinforce learning from past experiences, knowledge and responsibility

5. Methods of promoting excellence in execution within the appropriate level of authority and responsibility

The end result of these functional consequences of your organizational structure is a person who is a contributor to individual and organizational success.

QUESTIONS TO CONTEMPLATE

Q-1. What are the psycho/social consequences to each of the functional consequences of organizational structure? In other words, think about how a person feels and responds to organizational structure. To answer this question, begin each answer with "I'm _____". Tell me what an employee feels when faced with the five functional consequences of organizational structure (hint: high self-esteem and high regard for others is the end result).

1.

2.

3.

4.

5.

Q-2 What are the resultant behavioral traits of the Organizational Operating System?

Go to www.mcclureconsultants.com under literature and click on "Matrix for Improvement" for help.

# 4

## *Encourage Employee Ownership*

Think about what it takes to get people to take ownership in something. What keeps marketing and sales people always ready to accept the next challenge and, in effect, improve their performance over the previous quarter? Facing new challenges does not come naturally for sales people. In fact, they can be some of the biggest skeptics of all. But how do they get over the skeptical stage and focus on the task at hand? I believe that employees who can embrace change can also buy in to the possibility that their company offers value that is worth consuming. In other words, they become consumers of what their companies offer them.

Consumers look for the usefulness of a product or service to determine what need it meets and how much value it holds for them. A business looks for consumer needs to meet. As corporate leaders, we look for ways to make our product or service useful to our customers so they feel that they get maximum value from it. If we have done our job, the consumer then enters into an exchange where they trade consideration for the product or service (a value exchange). The medium used in the exchange is usually cash. The transaction is the exchange of cash for perceived value in the product or service.

Billions of marketing dollars are spent annually on influence to cause these transactions of exchange. There are three areas of concentration where influence has some effect. They are:

- Affect (the way we feel and our emotions)
- Cognition (the way we think about things)
- Environment (in what setting we prefer to make the transaction).

Business firms are also consumers. They expect to gain usefulness from all the resources they acquire in order to produce their product or service. Whether it is electricity, water, steel, lumber, land, or whatever the resource may be, the firm expects to utilize these resources in a consistent manner to create value. It is assumed that the electricity, water, and steel, etc., have a certain standard of quality, and a vendor must provide adequate capacity to deliver that quality on a consistent basis. Otherwise the firm will not receive maximum utility (usefulness) and consequently may decide to no longer make the exchange transaction with its present source.

In the same way, firms expect to gain utility from human capital—the people. How is employment a transaction of exchange? Usually, it is cash in exchange for the firm's consumption of their employee's time, talent, skill sets, education, experience, values and behavior. These attributes, when fully engaged, provide maximum utility for the firm's human resource consumption. The issue becomes the quality and the capacity to deliver the consistent level of usefulness from these resources purchased in the exchange. The goal for the firm is to gain the highest utilization of human capital by creating "value" in the exchange. Not just cash for time, but something of value for the maximum utilization of time, talent, knowledge, education, experience, values and behavior.

So consider how we get our customers to buy our products or services. We make a great product, we help our customers think about and feel how our product will meet their need, and we price it in such a way that they see value and are willing to exchange their money for our product. In a similar way, we help our sales people buy into our new sales plan.

So, as a manager, you should perceive your employees as your customer who is buying your product. What product? Bottom line, you are asking them to be consumers of your plan in exchange for their time, talent, experience, and knowledge, and desired behavior. Of course, they receive money for their services, but money is not all that will motivate them to stay. Other firms offer them money for their value exchange too.

To benefit from human capital, your employees should become consumers of your vision and mission of the organization—they need to "consume" or buy into what you are doing, how you do it, and for whom you do it. They need to feel ownership in what they do; their work needs to fulfill their own goals in order to stay motivated. Employees are willing to exchange their time, talent, experience and knowledge when they are confident they will have an appropriate level of control over their part of the value creation and the opportunity to earn adequate compensation. They will take ownership in their particular job if they see how it brings value in helping your bottom-line results.

When employees are willing to help make their company be profitable because of what they receive from the exchange, they understand the costs involved in ownership. Costs such as

- attending meetings
- planning and accountability to managers
- budgeting
- quarterly training exercises
- dealing with customers' and their demands just to name a few.

Sales people are consumers when they take ownership in your sales plan and decide to meet or exceed their forecasted sales budget. The value proposition for them comes from "buying into" the biggest cost of all—constant change—constant improvement. Every quarter, you ask them to change from what they know and are doing to something different, in order to continuously improve their performance and, consequently, your bottom-line results. You also ask more of them one year to the next by increasing their sales targets. You ask them to be consumers of corporate change and growth, and in so doing, find value in what they do. What is the value? It may be different for each individual, but it's going to range from a nice income all the way to an expression of self-actualization.

# INSPIRE YOUR EMPLOYEES AS CONSUMERS

If you view your employees as consumers, how do you market to them? How do you advertise your benefits? Consider how you get sales people to consume change.

Most companies send sales people into a location where they can associate with other sales people and spend time trading stories and experiences that will help each other. This is a time to build new connections and re-kindle established relationships. It is the ultimate environment for good communication.

Next, are briefings by the executive management team to provide the sales people with perspective on current trends in the industry, what is the planned response, what new things are in the pipeline, and what kind of opportunity it represents to them in future compensation.

The next day, the marketing department gives an overview of the market analysis and updates competitive intelligence. They also introduce and display new collateral materials for the products to be emphasized in the next quarter and give an overview of how to most effectively use them against the competition.

Finally, they have a banquet and recognize the efforts of top performers as well as presenting them with awards to commemorate their efforts. A speaker during the evening meal brings focus to the time spent over the course of the meeting and ties together neatly the reminder of what is expected of them over the next quarter. The evening usually ends with a question and answer session that drifts into a time of social mixing that reinforces the future (even if it is only for one quarter at a time).

At this point, the salesperson is able to take ownership of their future. The vision is in place for the new quarter, and the salesperson knows exactly what to do to achieve the mission. But how often does management impart the same level of information about future goals with the rest of the company?

Until *all* employees are convinced that changes are both right and reasonable and will deliver value to their own lives, they will resist change. As a manager wanting employee action, you must keep communication flowing to all departments because they will not make changes (act on the plan) until they know, understand, and believe that the changes will add value for them and for the greater good. All employees must understand their role in the scheme of the bigger picture and clearly understand the expectations placed on them to succeed.

For salespeople, the flow of information is a content-rich environment, meaning management is careful to paint the big picture allowing them a view of the future market. They ascribe appropriate value to the firm and to their position in relation to the overall market. Imagine how focused your workers would be if they were reinforced by learning from the executives in this way. Changes would finally make better sense, and they would buy in to their own role and responsibilities to make improvements happen. They would understand why you put the expectations on them that you do.

And what if communication doesn't happen? What if everyone besides Sales and Marketing lacks knowledge, understanding, belief, and action? If all your employees have the same benefit of input, they will join you in the task of striving for results to keep up with consumer needs.

Realize that the greater the change (the more effort required in doing something differently), the greater the need for knowl-

RANDY McCLURE

edge to compare solution alternatives. In other words, people want to know why they are being asked to change, and understand and believe that the change alternative is the best one for them and is a solution for the unmet need.

An effective way the marketing department achieves its goal of communication is to hold symposiums and roundtable discussions. The information of these sessions is then shared through a video with the field sales people. These discussion groups tackle the issues in solution alternatives and the marketing department builds its communication around that platform. Their involvement makes it easy for them to change. In fact, it is easy to continuously change and therefore improve their performance.

These same methods should be used to equip employees throughout the corporation, thus motivating them to continuously improve and change their ways to make themselves more valuable to your customers.

## MOTIVATE YOUR CAST OF PLAYERS

The workplace is like a theatrical play where the producer (the owner, or the executives), the writers (mid-level managers), and directors (supervisory management) all have input into the play. The audience (customers/market) never sees the input—they only see the actors' (customer service, accounts receivable, and sales personnel) value of the input. Actually, customers see only the results of actors' interpretation and value of the director's input.

Keep in mind that as a corporate leader, you are the producer and director and you give guidance and motivation to your actors, but in the end it is the actors' skill, experience, education, values, and personality that determine his or her performance.

How an actor translates the part being played is a result of

- training
- understanding of the role
- perception of the writer-director-producer
- the value placed on the role in light of the overall production
- the actor's own unique style (personality, values, attitudes).

It seems reasonable that when an owner/leader (the writer in our theatre analogy) decides that a strategic need for the firm is to launch an initiative to position itself as a world-class organization, that the team of executives (the producers) with whom he/she is surrounded would give valuable input that would become the structure of how that vision will be accomplished. The visionaries of leadership should hand-off to managers/supervisors (the directors) the job of planning out the processes and assigning the tasks to the players (the actors). Ultimately, the players translate the assigned tasks into completing the initiative. So workers need as much information as possible to fulfill their drive to know, understand, believe and act on the new strategy. When they feel they need more information, it should be easy for them to seek after and find.

Consider what happens to the audience—the customer—when all the actors of a play are fully engaged in their production. What happens if the actors seem disoriented, confused, and unsure of their roles? Which performance do you want your customers to see? Take steps to see that all levels of your team are equipped for the change (the new strategy).

As the owner/leader, you definitely have the customer or market in mind when forming a strategy around becoming world-class. You are convinced that the strategy meets and probably exceeds perceived customer expectations. But do your executives understand the strategy as well?

Ask for feedback and watch for signs of hesitation if your team is second guessing the degree of difficulty of administering such an immense task. Notice if any of your executives seemed affected by peer pressure to conform to a certain view, thus choking out the original intentions of your vision. Don't move on until you feel your first level of executives have the information they seek, know the precise plan (and acknowledge the need for it), understand and comprehend the strategy to achieve the goal, find the value of the changes proposed both right and reasonable, and are ready to act on the plan.

Then consider your managers and supervisors. Each executive is to communicate new goals to managers and supervisors. Require feedback to evaluate what percentage of the leader's vision is understood. Do any of the managers/supervisors just not get it? Is there a lack of full comprehension in comparison to the leader's comprehension? If yes, does that diminish the value of the leader's vision? Of course not! But how will that value be realized without everyone working to achieve the vision?

Obviously, if the value of the vision is not realized and is not acted on, then that opportunity becomes void. What was the cost of this lost opportunity?

If a strategy does not ignite, first look at your managers and supervisors to see if your vision became diluted by the time it reached their ears. How much of the plan can they explain back to you? Is it 25 percent? Less? More? What about their workers? How many of them comprehend the vision? If your goal has been handed down in a diluted portion, what will it take for them to believe it is right and reasonable, aligning their personal values behind it, and acting on what they believe to be a solid vision?

We have already seen evidence that sales people are able to quickly adapt to new plans and stay on task to accomplish goals because they have a clearer sense of your vision. So what might dilute the vision to the rest of the workforce and cause a void in place of opportunity? The difference is behavior based on attitudes! Salespeople quickly understand that their attitude helps them convince customers to buy. What if everyone in the workplace adopted the same outlook?

Attitudes by their nature cause people to bias the way they think and how much they comprehend. As we know, attitudes are formed around personal values, and it is through addressing these values that we find the kind of response we want. In the case of your corporate changes, how do employees value (esteem) your vision of becoming a world-class company? How do you relate to their personal values in order to help them see the need for change?

## INSPIRE GREAT ATTITUDES— SUCCESS WILL FOLLOW

Perhaps the need to equip your force with SKUBA (Seeking, Knowing, Understanding, Believing and Acting) gear is starting to make sense to you. When you first shared the vision of becoming a world-class organization, your executives immediately evaluated your plan with an affective (emotional) response. This response was based on their emotions, feelings from past experiences, and the immediate environment. They used their cognitive (thinking) skills and their emotions to form an immediate response to your vision.

Forming an initial good or bad attitude toward your plans happens quickly, so it is imperative that you overcome any doubts they may have at your initial presentation. You can do this by satisfying their need to seek more information, know (or acknowledge the need for what your vision accomplishes), understand, and believe in the solution before expecting them to simply act on the new plan. This integrated approach gives them personal relevance to your vision and determines whether your outcome will be a response that is favorable or unfavorable.

Fortunately, once this attitude forming process has occurred it is no longer necessary to repeat the integration process regarding the vision because the attitude is stored in memory. In other words, the response to the vision has been recorded and will be played back each time it is recollected. From this point on, every time the vision is mentioned the "memorized" response is front and center in the executive's mind. Consequently, your message with its potential benefit to be realized and the key to the heart of your listener (the listener's values) are all involved in the implementation of your vision.

The initial attitude conveyed at the point of delivery of a vision will shape ongoing operations. People inside the organization seek information, knowledge and understanding so they can determine (believe) whether or not to act on the changes required for improvement. Their attitudes toward change dramatically improve when they have SKUBA gear.

By now, I trust you understand the source of noise in your company. Obviously, the best written memo delivered via email or tacked to the corkboard in the break-room certainly pales by comparison to what should be communicated personally through the enthusiasm of leadership. New strategies should always be personally announced by someone:

- whose attitude is eager to seek improvement
- knows the plan well
- understands it enough to answer the questions of those who are just hearing the vision
- believes in its potential
- who is eager to act to make it happen.

Remember, how people process information when they first hear it will make a lasting impression on their attitude needed to carry out the plan. People will not act on what you ask them to do unless they believe that it is right and reasonable. You can coerce employees to do something different by threatening their job security, or you can provide incentive for them to do something different; but if these methods are used and real "buy-in" isn't happening, there will continue to be noise. [Beware: people are adept at hiding their true response so that others cannot perceive their initial reaction so you cannot rely on body language or facial expression alone.]

Experts agree that it only takes seconds for a first impression to occur. Good communication planning will increase a favorable first impression.

## AVOID BUYER'S REMORSE

The ultimate dissonance (or noise) is buyer's remorse. A consumer makes a purchase only to return home and realize they do not want the item after all. The cost of the item determines how much noise the customer will experience. Consider with me, for a moment, the last time you purchased toothpaste, soap, and tissues. You probably didn't take too long to make up your mind about which brand, and even from which store, you would choose to make the purchase. Right?

Now consider the last car you purchased. How long did you think about that car before you said: "I'll take it"? Why did it take you longer to buy a car than toothpaste? The alternative choices to that car became much more significant than the alternatives to the personal items. Was all of the information you needed to make the final decision on the car handed to you, or did you spend some time on the internet and looking through manufacturer's catalogues and other sources of information?

I'm sure you would agree that getting more information alone doesn't always result in your making a purchase. Most likely, you had an obvious need or you wouldn't have been looking for cars in the first place. At what point in the process did you know it was time to buy?

When I bought a car, first, the price had to fit my budget and of course I needed to make sure that the warranty would cover me through the years that my children were in college because with their expenses, I knew my budget could not afford to pay for any car repairs. I ordered one of those reports that lists dealer's costs on models and became thoroughly familiar with it so I could negotiate a good price. Also, it was important to me that the car had side air bags. Some of the models had them that year and some did not. I also remember wanting to make sure that road noise was not going to be a problem because we had a trip planned that year and I wanted to know that I could drive in relative quiet. I guess the last thing was the terms of the financing. I wanted to make sure I could get the appropriate discounts promised and with good terms.

Then what? Then I had confidence in my decision because it seemed right and reasonable to make an offer, and I went into the dealership and told the salesman what I would need as options and made him the offer.

What gave me the confidence to make a final purchase? When I finally made up my mind what I was going to do, I just did it. I'm not really sure at what point I felt confident. But now you may be wondering what does all of this have to do with the corporate noise or dissonance?

My steps in purchasing a car are similar to the processes your employees make when considering your request for them to change. Once I had the confidence to make the offer for what I was willing to pay, I also had the confidence to make a change and with that change I had fairly steep costs associated. At some point in my car-buying journey, I was able to find value in a particular model with particular features at a particular price. I had gained knowledge that helped me come to that point, but not without first going through a discovery process (seeking). Discovery and knowledge are key to getting people to accept change and to affect their actions.

When I was seeking more information about that car, I also looked up information about other car models and their features as well as other dealerships that carried the same model in which I was originally interested. I think if someone would have handed me all the information on the model I bought, it would not have satisfied my need to discover the whole picture on my own.

That's it! The key to my confidence that led me to "buy in" to a certain manufacturer's model was the fact that I had *sought* (discovered) more information on my own, and I *knew* my alternatives—not only in preferred models, but also in the sources of the same model. Now I had the basis for *understanding* the real need, a reasonable solution to my need, the alternatives within the solution, and their associated costs. I did not make the offer to buy what that dealer had to sell until I had all of that. I believed I had a good deal and so I acted and bought the car. Your employees need SKUBA gear to believe your planned change will meet their needs and the needs of your customer. As the leader, you are the one with the answers to satisfy the consumer needs of both your employees and your ultimate customer.

## CHAPTER FOUR – ACTIVITY

### QUESTIONS TO PONDER

*[Adapted from: Consumers, Eric Arnould, Linda Price, George M. Zinkhan copyright © 2003 The McGraw–Hill Companies]*

1. Describe a choice that you have made in each of the following categories:
   a. A career choice
   b. A low-involvement consumer choice
   c. A high-involvement consumer choice
   d. A choice relating to your friends
   e. An academic choice

Consider:
   How are these choices alike? How are they different?

2. Look at some ads in a magazine that you usually read. Try to identify whether they have a primary goal to influence
   a. cognitions (the way you think)
   b. emotions (the way you feel)
   c. actions (your behavior)

Consider:
   Which type is most effective on you? Which type is most effective on someone you know?

3. Think of an important decision that you have made.
   a. How did you make that decision?
   b. What role did thought, situation, or gut feelings play in this decision?

4. Find a website that helps consumers evaluate one brand at a time. Now find a website that helps consumers compare brands, one attribute at a time. Evaluate how these different websites might influence consumer decision making.
Describe how this translates to the workplace where:
   a. employees are given specific but limited amounts of communication
   b. employees discover the big picture but receive very little detail communication

# 5

## Quiet the
## Noise Level

As a management consultant who helps corporate leaders strategize top-line and bottom-line growth, I have observed three types of employees that need special attention in order to overcome the dissonance they may feel. At the beginning of this book, we looked at Bob (not his real name), who quit his job when offered a promotion. His attitude robbed him of the benefits of change. He only saw the task being offered as more work than he wanted to handle.

To continue the scenario in chapter one, something valuable was snatched away from Bob because he lacked a full comprehension of a great opportunity that lay before him. Steve was able to see that the new position offered value to

Bob, but the value was not realized. What seemed valuable to Steve was not valuable to Bob because he did not comprehend, leaving him unable to believe that the promotion was valuable. This is an important lesson in managing good people.

Steve should seek to know and understand what is valuable to Bob before expecting him to buy in to the change that he proposed. If Steve would have tied Bob's values to the proposed change, Bob could have believed and acted on the promotion offered. Bob didn't see value in the change so he didn't see it as an opportunity. Obviously, if the value of something isn't realized and is not acted on, it is a lost opportunity and sometimes a costly void.

It is easy to see that Bob simply didn't *understand* the value of his new role. Bob's attitude robbed him of comprehending the meaning of the vision, and his part in it, because it required change and he was not prepared for *how* to make the change. He didn't *seek* answers to the questions he had; he didn't consider trying to gain more *knowledge* (greater perspective) of the new role, he didn't even attempt to *understand* why he had been chosen for the new position and what it would require of him. He was unable to *believe* in its value, so he didn't *act* on the opportunity. Bob quit because (in effect) he didn't like being told he had to change.

How could this have been avoided? Maybe there were distractions. With Bob, there seemed to be no conscious awareness of the value of the vision and therefore no way to profit from it. What were the possible distractions? Wrong attitudes may have been formed in the proposal of the change. Whatever it was that distracted Bob from understanding the opportunity also diluted the full benefit of the vision for everyone involved. Bob's absence left a void that took considerable time to fill.

Then there is Joe (no, this isn't his real name either). As soon as Joe learned about proposed changes, he immediately made the attempt to understand them. But soon a small conflict arose and he retreated quickly to his old way of thinking. It is stunning to watch an associate still struggle with sticking to a plan even when he seems to clearly agree with the purpose of a new method. Joe was missing something that would have helped him stick through the trials of change. Whenever he meets difficulty in the middle of a new process, he quickly retreats to the old ways and abandons ship. He never lets the new way get a chance to establish roots. Joe didn't believe in the new methods enough to sort out the obstacles of necessary changes.

And what about Jack (also renamed)? Nothing ever really gets through to him. He says all the right stuff, and even gets involved in all the right activities that are expected of him, but he never seems to communicate the vision correctly when talking about it to others. Jack sounds like a company man and acts like he is willing to support management and contribute to the company's success, but the only thing that seems important to him is making enough money to keep his status in the community. He is more concerned with his reputation than making things better for the company and its customers. As long as he has the title and the salary, he'll say and do the things he has to in order to keep the status quo.

If only Bob, Joe, and Jack would adapt to the corporate vision like Paula. She not only understood the vision, she applied the principles and she saw real dividends paid. In meetings, she presented some materials that offered clear evidence she had fully incorporated the essence of the vision and the response from her audience was interesting. Some of the associate employees lightly heckled her over some detail, but Paula, not at all shaken, shared some amazing insight; before the meeting was over, the perspective Paula had shared was both enlightening and profitable to everyone present. Many left that meeting with newly shared values that rippled through their departments.

In my mind there is a correlating ratio between Paula's understanding of the vision and the effectiveness of everything she does. The more she understood and gained her own perspective on the corporate vision, the more her personal performance and productivity increased. She also seemed to be uniquely gifted to do the work she engaged in and enjoyed doing the work. The deeper Paula understood the vision, the more she did with it. When Paula was compared to the productivity of Joe and Jack, Paula's performance was consistently better.

It was clear that Paula's momentum was cyclical. The more she applied the principles of SKUBA, the more understanding she gained from her perspective which led to greater application, which led to greater perspective, which led to ongoing personal success. Positive change feeds itself. Conversely, the employees who made little effort to really understand the vision of change—enough to make it a "heart" matter tended to fade out. Over time, they even seemed to lose what little understanding they may have had when they began.

After a meeting, I once spoke with Paula about the vision that had been presented and her response was interesting to say the least. She said: "Once I comprehended my own personal need for the change required in the new vision, I knew I had to act on it. Although the vision is bigger than just me, it had to make sense on a personal level in order for me to act on it."

I asked Paula to explain when it was that she believed it to be valuable enough to act on it, and she replied: "I think what really occurred was that it finally seemed the right and reasonable thing to do."

"Do?" I asked.

"Yes," she replied. "Once it seemed like the vision was the right thing to do and a reasonable way to get it done, only then was I able to act on it and begin applying what I understood of the plan."

It was after hearing Paula reflect on what motivated her to adopt change that it became clearer to me there is no magic formula to make people understand and respond to a corporate vision, but I began to see the pattern of sustainable change in the workplace. Paula referred to the five essential elements of change that I now call SKUBA gear: seeking, knowing, understanding, believing, and acting. These elements create a pattern for success—a pattern in the sense of a roadmap. You do not have to start a trip at the beginning of a map, but you begin from where you are currently. In this case, whatever level of understanding one has of a corporate vision, a quarterly sales plan, or any planned change, it must seem right and reasonable before they will seek more information, before acting on what is understood.

At one point, Paula's level of understanding of the vision led her to seek more knowledge. It makes sense that the more she understood of the vision and her role in it, the better she comprehended the opportunity. In fact, the more she knows about the market, her customers and their ways, and any other change-agent for that matter, the greater her comprehension and the clearer it becomes to her that the vision is right, and reasonable. When it is right and reasonable, the only thing left to do is to take action according to what she knows and comprehends.

Would Paula's response to comprehending the opportunity satisfy her with what she knew and understood, or would it drive her to want to know more? As the value of something increases, we tend to want more information before we make the purchase (or make the change). In fact, I asked Paula how much time she spent thinking about the opportunity, and in her wisdom he replied, "We seek what we value."

I asked her to tell me a little more about that and she said: "In seeking valuable things like a better job, higher income, or more security, we plan, scheme and visualize ways to obtain them. People usually spend their resources [time, money, and effort] when seeking better things. It costs us something to pursue what we value."

Paula then shared that her favorite example of the ultimate pursuit of value or treasure is that of a miner digging in the earth for precious gems and minerals. Her key point is that much effort is needed for seeking and discovering value, no matter what form the value takes. She goes on to make the analogy that large mining operations incur huge expenses to recover only nominal amounts of payload, but the payload is extremely valuable with each ounce worth hundreds or even thousands of dollars. She says in the same way a mining operation incurs costs, it may also cost us some resources (primarily our time and focused attention) to uncover the "payload" in an opportunity, and we will only do this if we have properly valued the opportunity.

Consider for a moment what precious gems go through as a process to be revealed so that their full value is realized. Massive rock crushers begin the process and then grinders proceed to sift those nuggets. After grinding these smaller pieces of rock, the ultimate valuable gem is sawn, sanded, polished, and mounted in a setting to realize its full potential. Full refinement produces full value. The same is true with a corporate vision (or plan for change). The higher the level of the search for the vision's meaning and purpose, the more payload (perspective) it produces.

It's important to remember that some level of *understanding*

RANDY McCLURE

in the beginning of a vision is also the beginning of its value process, and the greater the understanding (as in Paula's case), the greater the value is appreciated; and the greater the value, the more we realize the importance of the search and discovery process. As Paula searched for more value in the corporate vision, she found it and acknowledged the value in all of her work.

To bring it all back to what it means, let's look at how Paula may have responded to the vision of becoming world-class company. Paula, hearing the world-class vision for the first time, responds to her immediate level of understanding by considering whether it seems right and reasonable to her. It does, so she *seeks* out her role and the anticipated resources needed to begin working on the task of carrying out her role. After applying what she *understands*, she senses the need to know more about what it means specifically to her role in the company.

Paula's search and discovery begins by asking questions and spending as much time as possible getting to *know the essence of the vision and the intentions of those who crafted it.* The more she knows, the greater her level of understanding becomes. With greater understanding comes Paula's self-check: "Is it right and reasonable?" If yes, then she acts on it. If at this point, the internal test for right and reasonable says, "No!" then, the only response would be for her to continue searching to know more about the vision and expectations for her role in it.

## HOW TO SELL YOUR VISION

Let's review this train of thought. People must first become aware that there is a need to improve performance in serving the customer. After they are aware, it is important that they are allowed to seek and discover information about the need, and know firsthand that there is value in fulfilling that need. They then must comprehend the solution you are proposing to meet that need and any associated costs involved to include what effect it will have on them personally. If that does not satisfy them, and they want more information, they need access to a content-rich environment where they can gain perspective along with more information. It is also important to allow for exploration of solution alternatives to be considered; once this step is complete, the value proposition will be clear and they will feel what you are asking them to do is right and reasonable.

So how do you get your employees to seek and discover, and to gain knowledge and understanding of your goals? How do you encourage them to acknowledge your vision as the change agent? Stop and think about it, when you know someone well, your emotions, feelings, and thoughts are more finely tuned to that person's needs and their ways. The better you know them (have intimate care and concern about them), the more you think about them. It's natural that when they enter your thoughts, they trigger emotional responses. You may even think of them during an event or a situation that somehow reminds you of them. This is acknowledging their essence, their personality, and their ways. How many of your employees do you know in this way? How many of your employees know you in this way? You need more than a casual co-worker connection with them. Obviously, a simple "Hey, how's it going?" is better than the stoic bluntness of a cold, "hello." But those whom you know well (personally, intimately) are usually greeted with a warmer and deeper sense of care, and this is the relationship you need to build with those whom you want to buy in to your vision.

In the business case, it is how well your employees know

and acknowledge the vision of being world-class in all that they do. This acknowledgement needs to pervade every part of what they do and how they carry out their roles. Their environment should be set up to remind them or prompt them to consider the essence of the vision. Paula is a great example of someone who has embraced an intimate knowledge of the corporate goal, and it is tempting to think that if you had ten more people just like her you would have it made. The point is, there are at least ten more people in your company that want to understand clearly your vision, and would willing apply their talents to helping you if they could see the value in doing so.

By now, you can see the pattern that is taking shape. The more focus given to the essential elements of seeking, knowing, understanding, and believing, the more one is convinced to act on what has been discovered. However, you can probably see that practicing these five elements of organization success is not a one-time effort; rather it calls for repeating those elements over and over again. There can be no end to it—you will never be done with SKUBA. But that's what makes it a pattern for success and not a formula.

I trust it has helped you to identify these essential elements as a platform for change in order to help your organization improve its performance. I want you to know how to capitalize on this pattern for change. Successful organizations will be those that can quickly respond to their environment (market) and to their competition. Therefore, it is critical to know how to introduce change so that employees respond like Paula, and not like Bob, and work toward the common goal.

# MORE ON FORMULAS, ROAD MAPS, AND PATTERNS

Many times when someone presents a "formula" for success, the result brings disaster. Disaster in that the original intent was not accomplished. And to add insult to injury, people were left less than enthused (to say the least) about ever trying something new again. As I mentioned before, the elements of change that I have presented to you do not offer a formula for success, but a pattern for effective leadership to positive change in the workplace.

Those who attempt improvement as a formula must realize that a formula is merely a template for arranging information, and formulas are usually part of equations that give a conclusive result. Whether it is addition, subtraction, multiplication, or division, the effect of the formula always concludes in a sum total. The "formula-for-improvement" approach comes down to doing certain types of work in a certain way every time to conclude with a certain result. It is very mechanical, and can seem almost robotic.

Nike's "Just Do It!" slogan doesn't apply here. In fact, any advice that contains the word *just* might be suspect after you consider the previous sections in this book. Just plan more, just work harder, just do more, just try more, just learn more, just . . . just . . . just . . . get the picture? Positive change has more to do with the personal exchange of information than expecting everyone to just do something and its benefits can be seen repeatedly in peoples' eager responses to participate.

The platform for improvement that management desires is already at work in each of their people, and that is how SKUBA gear differs from a formula and how we keep ourselves engaged in the real meaning of change for the purpose of improvement. The five elements of SKUBA are not a formula—not just a plan, not a method, not an approach, but a pattern of behavior representing a proper response toward the need for change.

As with a map, you don't always start at the beginning of the picture. You must find out where you are in relation to the map and begin from that point. If you were in Atlanta and wanted to go to Boston, it wouldn't seem wise to travel to Los Angeles to begin your trip just because the map appeared to begin in Los Angeles. As in following a pattern, you would start from where you are, and begin your trip in Atlanta and then follow the map instructions to Boston.

It is the same with following the SKUBA pattern for change to improve your workplace. You start where you are in the pattern and begin there. Perhaps your employees still need knowledge or to acknowledge the agent of change. Maybe they don't quite believe in your plan for change. Then you need to find new ways to allow them to go through the discovery process to find what they need to know and understand before they can fully buy in to what it is you are asking of them.

SKUBA is a pattern for change. Unlike a formula with specific steps, a true pattern has no beginning, and no end. Instead, it repeats itself over and over and never concludes.

Some software applications allow the user to discover trends and patterns in the data, which are often helpful for predicting outcomes. The better the trends and patterns are understood, the better the outcomes are predicted. Desired outcomes are achieved by emphasizing certain elements in the pattern.

So how does this relate to how people feel about the work you expect from them? First, you need to identify the mix of elements that result in your employees becoming good consumers of what you are selling. Remember the elements: Seeking, Knowing, Understanding, Believing, and Acting (SKUBA).

## CONCLUSION

The natural place to begin in the pattern of corporate improvement is through raising the level of understanding that your employees currently have about your goals and your market. Realize that all employees want to feel as though they are "in" on what is going on at their work. Build their understanding by offering knowledge of your vision, goals, and plans.

You have learned about SKUBA gear to find out how to improve your company. You sought information, you read the examples to know what is needed, you now understand the need for thorough communication with your employees, and you believe that this is an effective pattern for progress. Now it's your turn to act and teach your employees to thrive in their work. Show them how to escape boring, routine, monotonous work by using SKUBA gear to embrace positive change. Encourage seeking because it sets up the process for discovery, and help others to acknowledge you (and your vision) as the change agent because it is essential for learning better ways to stay competitive in your market.

In relation to the overall effectiveness of meeting goals or pursuing strategy, critical thinking is under-utilized in managing one's work. Managers are expected to be good critical thinkers in analysis and understanding trends, but too often, it is not expected of clerical or technical workers—yet they are the ones who own the process. Those closest to the work should be expected to look for ways to improve the way their work is done. This only happens if workers think like good managers in their own areas of responsibility.

Remember, to be a good manager of their own work, their most valuable resource is knowledge—not rocket science, but this truth is often ignored. In business, managers are often dealt the unexpected, and the best leaders manage chaos and ambiguity into order (opportunity). Effective managers will inform their team of a deliverable and then ask their employees to work their way backward through the processes which must occur in order to produce that deliverable. As employees seek answers, they will also gain knowledge as they explore ways to achieve the new goal. Employees begin to believe in themselves and what they are doing as they discover new methods to take the company where its leaders want it to go.

It is good that employees are required to deal with ambiguity through critical thinking. It allows them to understand the chaos. Understanding the chaos comes from determining the variables and how they relate to each other, and the role each variable plays in the outcome (order). Overcoming the ambiguity plays a huge role in SKUBA. Most real-life situations do not present themselves with full detailed instructions and color slides informing the participant of exactly what to expect and what decisions to make.

Change is a life-long journey that will lead us on a path to becoming the very best we are designed to be. SKUBA leads to good choices that will impact not only our lives, but also the lives of those around us.

Corporate success requires everyone seeking [SEEKING] the treasures (nuggets of valuable insight and information) of your vision and of the market they are competing in, and acknowledging [KNOWING] the change agent—you or the customer, the organization or ideology requiring the change. It requires understanding [UNDERSTANDING] the relationship of their role and their resources to the development of strategy for change. Only when what they believe [BELIEVING] to be the right thing to do and reasonable as to cost and benefit for themselves and for the firm will they take action [ACTING] on what they understand and know. You now have a mix of five elements that, when applied, produces desired results. You know that the greater the understanding, the greater the value realized by all. So what are you doing to help everyone in your organization overcome resistance to change and understand (comprehend) the need for it, and to ensure that all get the benefit?

Understanding at any level is helpful. Of course, understanding requires new choices to be made. Either your employees will accept your message and trust it, or reject it and turn away. Some will naturally respond well to what you ask them to do. They most likely would see that what you are asking them to understand is at least valid. It's the next step that gets tricky. What they understand with their head must somehow move down to their heart (where values reside) in order for them to feel ownership of your vision. That's where real understanding makes a difference—and that requires clear and continuous communication from you.

In order to experience real transformation, a person must trust what they understand to be true in order to move it from their mind to their heart (believing) where it is allowed to change their behavior (acting). Deep, sustainable change is achieved when employees internalize or align their inner-selves (their personal values) to what they understand to be true. So if you want your organization to be transformed, write your vision for change in their minds and on their hearts, where it will take root and grow.

# DIVE IN WITH SKUBA CERTIFICATION

Training Program
Organizational Improvement with SKUBA

A note from the author . . .

This training is different from other business training in that it is multi-dimensional.
It deals with psychological, emotional, social and environmental conditions in the workplace.

- It is not a course that you memorize material and regurgitate on tests (it's too voluminous).
- It does not offer practicality of use in the same sense that accounting, marketing, or business law offer.

Accounting, Marketing, and Law are learned and then applied. Organizational Improvement concepts are applied, and then the learning begins. The best way to study an organization and its behavior is to be involved in the organization. It is unlike studying math or marketing or accounting where doing the related activities over and over is the best way to master the subject. In those subjects, problems are assigned and then worked to show progress in learning the material. In Organizational Improvement, situations (rather than problems) are assigned in order to observe the reality of the concepts presented.

Difficult to explain, but simply put: Organizational Improvement is about interaction. It's about people intersecting with others and making sense out of what they encounter. Because this training is different, the instructional methods and learning styles are different too.

A manager's most valuable resource is knowledge. The idea is to create the "best-of-thinking" in a way that facilitates best-in-class performance throughout a team or group. Applied in the business world this provides owners and managers with confidence in their firm's level of performance, and comfort in their level of control. Managers are expected to be good critical thinkers in analysis and understanding trends, but too often this expectation is not extended to workers—those who own the process. In relation to the overall effectiveness of meeting goals or pursuing strategy, critical thinking is an element of excellence in managing one's work. Those closest to the work should be expected to look for ways to improve the way work is done. This only happens if workers think like good managers.

The team-based exercises are carried out in projects. These scenarios are planned to build a set of experiences for you to reflect back on in order to gain perspective on the concepts of organizational improvement. So it is in retrospect that this training comes full circle.

Training Course Content
- Foundations of Change
- Individuals
- Groups
- Organizational Systems and Dynamics
- SKUBA

I hope the training is meaningful, and I thank you in advance for your attention and effort.
For more information contact us:
McClure Management Consultants, LLC, 1811 S. Baltimore, STE. 205, Tulsa, OK 74119
www.mcclureconsultants.com